Silver Hotrod

Goes To Daytona

Written by

Finn & Jake

Thanks to all our readers

Silver Hotrod was so excited to be at Daytona for the first time.

He'd heard there was a big race on and had come a long way to see it.

"Oh Boy! I can't wait!"

Silver Hotrod was bursting his pistons to get to the race.

But disappointment struck. All the tickets were sold out?

"Oh no! Now I can't go and see the best race ever!"

Silver Hotrod's tires were so deflated.

He turned around to go home, but two cars squished him like a waffle into the race track.

"HEY! STOP PUSHING!"

He stared at the stadium in awe.

A Race Official spotted him. "What's your name?" He roared.

"I'm Silver..."

He interrupted Silver Hotrod. "Oh, you're Silver Blazer. Here's your number. Now get to your starting place, we have a race to get going."

"But, but..."

But the Race Official was too busy to listen.

"Get to the grid, Silver, I gotta race to run!"

The crowd was cheering with great excitement.

Oh, no he, thought. Race these serious sports cars? I can't do it, how can I? But then I'll never get a chance to do this, ever again.

"I'm going to do it!" He shouted.

Silver Hotrod wasn't just at the Daytona race track, he was on it!

When he got into place, the other racing cars were roaring their engines. "VROOOM!"

"Maybe I should make a ton of noise too," said Silver Hotrod. He vroomed his engine!

"Are you ready to race!?" Shouted the flag car.

All the cars responded with a yes. "All right then. The race will start in 3...2...1...GOOO!" He said.

Then he wondered how he was going to get down from there...

All of the racers sped off, but Silver Hotrod was going slower than a snail.

"Why is he going so slow?" Said the cars in the audience.

Slime, slime...

Then Silver Hotrod remembered what Jimmy, the police car from Oilville had told him a month before.

"You're making too much noise, that's what's making you go slow!"

Silver Hotrod stopped making noise. He zoomed up to, and right through, the other racers.

"WOW!" Shouted the audience.

"WOW!" Roared the other race cars.

Before he could blink, Silver Hotrod had done 52 laps and won the race.

"Amazing!" Said the commentator. "The winner ain't always the one with the fastest car, it's the one who refuses to lose. And that's Silver!"

"We have a winner!" Said the owner of Daytona "Well done, Silver Blazer."

"Actually, my name is Silver Hotrod."

"Huh, we thought you were Silver Blazer, never mind. Silver Hotrod it is. You've won the race so here is the trophy and $500'000!"

The crowd went wild!

After a whole evening of celebration, Silver Hotrod left for home.

But little did he know, two cars were watching him, eager for a different type of race.

To be continued...
Hi Finn and Jake here, with a hint for Silver Hotrod Book 3.

Gold : Bronze, Bronze : Silver,
Silver : Gold

This is the end of the book. There's no reason to continue forward as there are no more pages! LOL...
Do tell us what you think on Amazon by leaving us a review please!
Thanks for reading. See you in book three!

Silver Hotrod

Finn and Jake

RED RIBBON WINNER
Wishing Shelf Awards 2017

Silver Hotrod
Bronze, Silver & Gold

Finn and Jake

Printed in Great Britain
by Amazon

21451027R00018